The Precious Gift

The Hymns, Carols, and Translations of Henry L. Lettermann

Compiled and Edited by
Scott M. Hyslop

Lutheran University Press
Minneapolis, Minnesota

The Precious Gift
The Hymns, Carols and Translations
of Henry L. Lettermann

Compiled and Edited by Scott M. Hyslop

Copyright © 2013 Scott M. Hyslop. All rights reserved. Published by Lutheran University Press, an imprint of 1517 Media. No part of this book may be reproduced or transmitted in any form by any means, electronic, mechanical, recording, or otherwise, without the express permission of the author. For information or permission for reprints or excerpts, please contact the author.

Published under the auspices of:
  Center for Church Music
  Concordia University Chicago
  River Forest, IL 60305-1402

ISBN-10: 1-932688-91-9
ISBN-13: 978-1-932688-91-7
eISBN: 978-1-942304-89-0

Contents

Acknowledgments 5
Introduction 7
Biographical Information 11
"Giving Wings to Prayer" by Christyne Lettermann 14
"Make It New: *Lutheran Worship* (1982)"
    by Henry L. Lettermann 19
Original Hymns, Carols, Sacred Texts, and Secular Poems 27
Translations of German Hymns 99
Background Notes on Hymns, Carols, and Translations 111
Index of Titles and First Lines 125

Acknowledgments

A project of this nature would be impossible to undertake without the assistance of many individuals. I am sure that I will forget to list someone to whom gratitude is due—for this I apologize—but I still feel the need to express thanks to various individuals for their assistance throughout the course of this project.

The following are people who have supplied me with hymn texts and background information on Dr. Lettermann's life and work: Dr. Paul Bouman, Dr. Carl Schalk, Dr. Ralph C. Schultz; the sainted Dr. F. Samuel Janzow, Dr. Paul G. Bunjes, Dr. Richard W. Hillert, Prof. Victor G. Hildner; the staff of Klinck Memorial Library at Concordia University Chicago; and Dr. Wayne Lucht.

My deepest gratitude and admiration are extended to Mrs. Betty Lou Lettermann-Kelly and her family for the numerous letters and phone calls over the course of this project. Betty Lou's enthusiasm, gentle sense of humor, and willingness to dig through her husband's files has made this project a joy to work on from beginning to end.

SOLI DEO GLORIA

Scott M. Hyslop

Henry Lettermann
ca. 1962

Introduction

The title for this anthology of original hymns, carols, and translations by Henry L. Lettermann is a verse from one of his original hymns on the Incarnation—"The Precious Gift." In this text Dr. Lettermann tells us that "In mystery the Father sends the precious gift of light. His Son, our substitute, descends, redeems us from the night." God's Son did descend into the darkness of our world to become a beacon of light, illuminating the path of our pilgrim journey. The hymns, psalms, carols, and songs which the church has sung throughout history are a sure sign from God, a reflection of Christ the Light of the world, which emanates from a loving, caring Creator whose Spirit has not forsaken the wandering pilgrims, but continues to light the path and gives new songs to sing along the way.

The hymns, carols, and translations of Henry Lettermann are ruggedly hewn, and well-crafted. They reveal an author who was astutely aware of the rich legacy of confessional, didactic, and scripturally sound hymnody which is the heritage of the Lutheran Church. Lettermann's ability as a craftsman and artist can be seen throughout his work, as it is a rare person who has the true gift to combine a sound theological understanding with an poet's sense of style, image and meter. Lettermann works with language in the same manner that a sculptor might work with metal or stone. He takes the raw material of God's word, working it so that its divine message is brought forward and elevated.

From an academic and historical perspective, Lettermann's texts show us how matters of language and poetic structure have dramatically changed in the world of hymnody over the course of the last half of the twentieth century. When Lettermann began writing his hymns, *The Lutheran Hymnal* (1941) was the primary source and model for those wishing to create new liturgical song and hymns within the Lutheran Church–Missouri Synod. His work clearly represents how one author and one church body grappled with issues of language used in worship during the last quarter of the twentieth century. It is fascinating to look over these texts and watch the transformation from the language of *The Lutheran Hymnal*, as reflected in some of Lettermann's early writing, to the leaner poetry of his later work, devoid of all "thees" and "thous" as well as capitalized pronouns referring to the Deity.

Lettermann's work culminated in the Missouri Synod's *Lutheran Worship* published in 1982. *Lutheran Worship* was as dramatic a departure from *The Lutheran Hymnal* as could be imagined at that time. Hymns, liturgies, and language which had been familiar to generations of worshipping Missouri Lutherans were now replaced with new, and in some cases, challenging materials. Some of these changes were very well done and have been embraced over time, while other changes, well intended as they may have been, fell short and became points of contention and irritation.

Now we are in the early years of a new century and millennium. The Lutheran church bodies in America are further apart than ever regarding issues of language in worship. A multiplicity of worship forms and styles confront and challenge mainline Protestant churches in ways that would not have been imagined even at the time of the launching of *Lutheran Worship* in 1982. These issues, which have exploded over the course of the past twenty-five years, have brought forth a difficult question for thoughtful clergy, musicians, poets, and laity—"What language shall I borrow to thank Thee, dearest Friend?"[1] While there is probably no definitive answer to this question, it is important to look at the writings and materials left to us by those have wrestled with this question before. As the saying goes, "You can't know where you are going unless you know where you have been," and even though some of what has come down to us from the past may appear to be over zealous and even parochial in approach, there are important lessons to be learned and important insights to be gained upon honest examina-

---

[1] "O Sacred Head, Now Wounded" (stanza three), *Lutheran Service Book* #449.

tion of the clear progression in Henry Lettermann's writing, which is a mirror of larger trends that were going on simultaneously in the church at large.

So why should we care about the work of Henry Lettermann at this point in time? Here are a few reasons:

1. His writing on the *process* of writing gives us a clear picture into the thinking of those individuals who were charged with providing new worship materials for one church body in the late twentieth century.
2. As has been mentioned, it is fascinating to see his own transition from his early writing, replete with *"these and thous,"* to his later, more transparent work.
3. It is important to understand that regardless of where the swinging pendulum that seems to regulate the church's worship life is positioned at this moment, Henry Lettermann's writing is in fact well-crafted and thoughtfully written poetry.
4. Henry Lettermann's poetic legacy includes hymns written specifically for the training and edification of children, original hymns intended for liturgical proclamation, as well as fresh translations of classic German hymns.
5. A quick survey of Lutheran hymnals shows us that his writing has been represented in four out of six Lutheran hymnals published since 1978:
    - 1978 *Lutheran Book of Worship* (ELCA)—contains no texts by Lettermann
    - 1982 *Lutheran Worship* (LCMS)—contains six original texts and five translations
    - 1993 *Christian Worship* (WELS)—contains two original texts
    - 1996 *Evangelical Lutheran Hymnal* (ELS)—contains one original text
    - 2006 *Evangelical Lutheran Worship* (ELCA)—contains no texts by Lettermann
    - 2006 *Lutheran Service Book* (LCMS)—contains two original texts by Lettermann

F. Samuel Janzow (1913-2001), a contemporary and colleague of Dr. Lettermann, wrote the following regarding the significance of Henry L. Lettermann's work:

> Henry L. Lettermann's finely wrought Christian songs, carols and translations are of high poetic and spiritual quality. Think of the light of a kerosene lamp on an old upright piano. Its light shines through a three-paneled transparency into a dark room so that what the children see there, they never forget. They see the radiance of the divine-human child in the manger of the central scene. The left and right panels radiate heaven's glory in the angelic messenger and choir, and the golden gleaming magi gifts. So also the humble, gentle, ever-serving, God-given faith and spirit of Dr. Lettermann shines in and through his work to glorify his God and Savior. Look, read, sing what he wrote: you will see how like a trusting child he grasps the Father's gracious hands and will not let go of the littlest finger of his words and promises. His hymnody is a transparency displaying God's love and grace in Christ toward him and for all, as well as his responding faith, hope and love toward the one living and three-personed God. God is revered. Worshipers, young, or old are edified. A darkling world can hear the clear witnessing. This is the high significance and eternal worth of the hymnody of Henry L. Lettermann.[2]

May the reflection of Jesus Christ the Light of the world, as revealed in the work of Henry L. Lettermann, continue to be a beacon of God's light and love for generations to come.

---

[2] Correspondence with the author, October 18, 1993.

Biographical Information

The youngest of four children, Henry L. Lettermann was born February 28, 1932, to Henry Christopher Lettermann and Anna (née Gerstacker) Lettermann, at Pittsburgh, Pennsylvania. His primary level education took place at First Evangelical Lutheran School in Sharpsburg, Pennsylvania, where his father served as principal. It was in this setting where the riches of the church's song would be imprinted on the young heart and mind of Henry Lettermann. After his education at First Lutheran, he attended Concordia High School ,matriculating to Concordia Teachers College (now Concordia University) in River Forest, Illinois, where he received the bachelor of science degree in 1954. It was at Concordia where Lettermann's love for literature and poetry, especially the poetry of Americans Walt Whitman, Emily Dickinson, and Robert Frost, began to be formed. With the encouragement and scrutiny of friends and professors, the young writer's work began to take root and grow.

While at Concordia one of the foremost influences on Lettermann was Arthur E. Diesing, professor at Concordia Teachers College from 1923 to 1958. In a tribute to Diesing, which appeared in the spring 1966 issue of *Motif*—a literary journal published by the faculty and students of Concordia, River Forest—Lettermann wrote the following words to honor a teacher who had profoundly influenced his own life and work:

> His (Diesing's) only fault was that he loved excellence inordinately. He could fix you with his penetrating demand that you "get to the point," and heaven help you if you had no point to get to. Yet his unrelenting pursuit of meaningful interpretation of the aesthetic inspired you to be dissatisfied with the superficial, the

"meretricious," and to learn to love the true with understanding.

This training in excellence, and the pursuit of meaningful interpretation would become fully apparent as Lettermann extended his talents into the world of hymn writing.

In 1953 Lettermann married Betty Lou Piotter, a union which was blessed with two children—Richard George (1954) and Christyne Hope (1956). Following his graduation from Concordia, Lettermann received a call to join the faculty of the Junior High School of Trinity Lutheran Church, Fort Lauderdale, Florida (1954-56). From there he moved to Lutheran High School Central in St. Louis, Missouri (1956-59). In 1959 he received a call to become instructor of English at his alma mater—Concordia College, River Forest. In 1959 Lettermann received his master of arts degree from the University of Chicago, subsequently receiving his doctor of philosophy degree from Loyola University, Chicago, in 1974. Eventually Dr. Lettermann achieved the rank of full professor at Concordia.

Lettermann's talent for poetry and his genuine interest in education resulted in a number of fruitful unions. A number of his texts appeared in the *Concordia Music Education Series,* published in the 1960s by Concordia Publishing House, while numerous hymns and carols appeared in *Lutheran Education*—the official journal of the Lutheran Education Association. From 1979 to 1987 Lettermann served as a member and secretary of the Hymn Text and Music Committee of the Lutheran Church–Missouri Synod's Commission on Worship which prepared *Lutheran Worship* (1982). As a member of this committee he contributed both original texts andtranslations from the German. As a servant of the church at large, Lettermann also wrote texts on commission from various congregations as well as individuals.

Complications from multiple sclerosis caused Lettermann to resign his professorship and seek early retirement in 1988. Restricted to a health care facility, Dr. Lettermann and his wife chose to spend his remaining days in Florida. Henry L. Lettermann passed away in late summer of 1996.

Henry Lettermann
with his granddaughter Heather
ca. 1982

Giving Wings To Prayer

In Memoriam
+ Henry L. Lettermann+
2/28/32 – 9/24/96

I was raised in a literary household, a veritable incubator for linguistic endeavors. Some of my happiest childhood memories revolve around family suppers which were festive occasions for creative storytelling, feeding my fertile young mind with lessons in puns, alliteration, onomatopoeia, symbolism, metaphor, paradox, and—above all—the invaluable place of humor as a safety valve in the expression of life's pain. I learned to value expressing images in the most precise of ways, always striving for exactly the subtle shading required to convey the essence of thought.

Both my parents had chosen teaching as their professional careers. My mother taught kindergarten and my father was a professor of English at Concordia Teachers College, as it was called in those days. My brother and I spent endless hours wandering around the campus as youngsters, learning all the secret passages known only to the buildings and grounds engineers, studying all the stuffed animals on display in the science building, and listening to future teachers practice piano or organ in the music building.

We lived in college-provided housing, a three-flat not far from the campus. While our household belongings reflected the early 1960s income of Lutheran schoolteachers with two kids, my father's greatest material possession was a baby grand piano, which the Spirit had sent our way. In addition to directing college plays and other duties routinely assigned to him, my father had the unusual good fortune to mingle creatively with some of the most talented Lutheran composers—most notably Carl Schalk and Richard Hillert, now of international fame. They composed church music and, when it came to writing texts, they often asked my father or his colleague, F. Samuel Janzow, to collaborate.

When my father was in the grip of his musing, it was palpable and audible to the rest of the family. He would sit at the piano and play the wordless composition over and over for hours, like Lady Macbeth washing her hands, sometimes stopping to jot down a phrase or two, but mostly I think he was mesmerized by the very life and spirit of the music, listening to the chording and tone, opening himself up to the creative inspiration about to be given to him. He would sometimes pace back and forth, fertilizing an idea in his head. Then he would return to the piano and play out a section, comparing the imagined jigsaw fit of a piece of text in his mind with the real, uncompleted puzzle on the music stand.

And then, usually in a matter of days, a penciled text would mysteriously appear on the dinette table, written on the reverse side of an old copy of a purple dittoed college course outline, completed by Dad in the wee hours of the preceding morning and left for my mom's critique. I remember discovering these poems first thing in the morning and I stopped to read them, too, but often the subtlety of his genius or the obscurity of his biblical reference missed its mark with my yet developing mind and soul. But each new citing spawned a celebration.

Dad would take the text to school with him and engage his literary colleagues in a round-table coffee break triage, discussing everything from choice of meter and words to images and themes. He would then refine and revise the text, and a final hand-written draft of the hymn would magically reappear on the dinette table, its apparent effortlessness betraying his labor-intensive process. And so it went with the dozens of hymns and carols he wrote during the years of my childhood.

Understanding well my part in the academic Lutheran legacy intended for me, it seemed only natural that I would fulfill my parent's expectation of becoming the third generation on both sides of the family to graduate from Concordia. Accepting that this pre-programmed destiny included a teaching career, where else should I receive my training but at the campus home I'd always known and loved? For a short time I was the envy of other freshmen who kept mistaking one campus building for another. But by my sophomore year, I had reached the decision that I was terrified at the prospect of maintaining classroom discipline, and I opted instead for matriculation in a liberal arts degree program. And to what else was I drawn but English as my major?

At this time, my dad became my teacher as well as academic advisor, and I have many fond memories of the classes I took with him. My "Modern Poetry" class sparkles like a rare gem in my educational brooch, in part because I believe my father demonstrated such a passion for poetry. For years, he and I had been having a long-standing debate about the validity of "all that meter junk"—as I had affectionately named the art of structured poetry—and I will never forget the moment he introduced the class discussion of meter by affectionately disclosing his daughter's favorite name for it.

In addition to analyzing the literary styles of some of the best modern poets like Walt Whitman, Emily Dickinson, and Robert Frost, my father had a way of getting beneath their style to the undergirding of meaning and theme. He espoused the philosophy that poetry had value on many levels, but that truly good poetry "sings eternal songs." Surely this had a special meaning for him in light of his own religious poetry.

In the late 1970s, my father was appointed a member of the Lutheran Church–Missouri Synod's Commission on Worship, which was responsible for updating and revising texts for its new hymnal. He participated in meetings scheduled in St. Louis, discussing text changes and debating which hymns among the many would be published as the chosen few. To my father's greatest joy, eleven of his original or translated texts appear in the hymnal, *Lutheran Worship*.

When my father was in his early 50s, he was diagnosed with multiple sclerosis, which took its toll on his teaching through diminished physical facility, decreased vision, deteriorated mental agility, and increased fatigue. For one so nimble at weaving literary tapestries, this relentless illness was voraciously vindictive. After teaching at Concordia for over thirty years, my father went on disability in 1988 and moved to Florida, where he and Mom had always planned on retiring. For several years, he was in a nursing facility, paralyzed and unable to speak. On rare occasions, his unfocused eyes still glistened when the conversation turned to Concordia, as some random electrical current in his brain magically entered the cortical labyrinth activating these memories, imprinted long ago upon his psyche as vividly as one's first adolescent love affair.

In those last few years, as I was preparing for his death, I struggled to understand my father as an adult. A child's view of her parents provides such limited insight into who they really are as people. My father was an intensely private person who veiled his deepest self. My quiet odyssey of discovery, muted by his introversion and the progression of his disease, has drawn me to search for him in those places where he has left his loudest self-expressions—in his poetry. But his hymns, like any artist's work, provide only a glimpse of his world as seen through his eyes at the point in time that the work was created. No more and no less. He leaves behind a legacy of spiritual poetry which bears witness to an enormous, almost childlike trust and faith in his God which one can only hope to still be the same for him today as when he wrote so passionately about it years ago.

And what shapes the faith of my father's daughter, and what influence does his poetry have on her? In many ways I am like him. I see my world through symbols and images and am fascinated by their relationship to meaning and value. My inner world is richly complex, and, being introspective, I often share my insights with others through writing. But most of all, I am grateful for his instilling in me the appreciation of aesthetic poignancy, sensitivity to nuance, and unquenchable thirst for discovering spiritual truth.

I would like to conclude with the words of Henry Louis Lettermann, from his poem entitled "At Evening":

Now has the weary sun slipped down to the sky,
Earth now is sleeping, and so soon shall I.

Father, I thank thee that during this day
Thy hand has led me in work and in play.

Father, forgive me the wrongs I have done,
Bless those I love and, Lord, bless everyone.

Then in Thy love I will rest through this night;
Lead, Lord, through the darkness and bring me to light.

Daddy, may your soul be at rest in God's eternal light. Amen.

Christyne H. Lettermann

"Make It New"

The following is excerpted from an article written by Dr. Lettermann for the January-February 1982 edition of Lutheran Education, *the official publication of the Lutheran Education Association. In this article Dr. Lettermann explains his process of updating and revising the hymn texts which appear in* Lutheran Worship (LW). *As issues regarding relevance and inclusivity of language were in their infancy at the writing of this article, Lettermann's article serves as a window into his mind regarding these issues as well as hymn writing in general. This article is reprinted by permission of the editor of* Lutheran Education.

Language: The strong feeling of the LCMS Commission on Worship (like that of the people who produced LBW [*Lutheran Book of Worship*]) was that to be effective, the language of worship must not be allowed to be separate from the language which is used every day by the worshipper. When these languages become different, separate from each other, one also is promoting an unhealthful separation of religion and worship from life. This is probably not true for people of mature age whose many meaningful spiritual experiences are (for them) inseparable from the hallowed forms of the language, but I would propose that it is progressively more true for most of us as time passes and as language inevitably continues to change. In addition, there are impeccable literary grounds: we live in a world different from that of our fathers of 1913. Though the spiritual realities have not changed, we have, and our language has, and a just embodiment of our experience of the spiritual realities is better met in materials of worship that reflect our own times and experiences. Why do new poems and novels continue to be written? One does not put new wine in old bottles.

Let me reflect another "prejudice" I have on this subject. I believe strongly that worship materials have a profound influence on the life and the faith that the church professes. It is in the forms of worship that one finds the living embodiment of the creeds and confessions of the church, and therefore one "tampers" with the forms of worship with great fear and trembling. Each generation must approach this ongoing evolution of its forms of worship with reverential orthodoxy, with theological acuity, with piety, and with prayer. And for perhaps many, any change in language hallowed by long use and meaningful experience will seem to be a kind of reductionism. (the other side of that is that new language might also invigorate, enliven, perhaps even supply new insight.)

Updating: This updating of language of the hymnody of LW is the only part of this complex subject that I can address with any degree of knowledge. Changes number in the thousands. To a great extent, the pronouns "thee," "thou," "thy," and "thine" disappear in the new hymnal. Archaic "King-Jamesian" words are altered. (I will never again have the completely harmonious relationship I once had with one of my colleagues in the English department, because I dared to suggest the alteration of the word "fain" in "Jerusalem, Thou City Fair and High"—"my longing heart fain, fain, to thee would fly"—because any alteration of this in no way meets with her approval.) The forest of capitalization which one finds in *The Lutheran Hymnal* has been reduced; crabbed and convoluted word orders have been smoothed and made to follow more naturally, though surely some still survive. (The dimensions of the problem are almost infinite.) The problem becomes most acute in hymnody when riming is involved. Could one consider altering "My faith looks up to thee/Thou Lamb of Calvary" (TLH, 394)? What happens to "Take my life and let it be/Consecrated Lord to thee" or "Take my will and make it thine/It shall be no longer mine" (TLH 400), when one has decided that "thee" should be "you" and "thine" should be yours? (The first thing I expect to hear is that the writers of LW are theological liberals whose intention it was to subvert the theology of the church and corrupt the morals of the young.) Nor do any linguistic arguments (even if they are valid) change the feeling that the hymn book has been violated.

For instance, "thee" and "thou" and "thine" and "thy" were used precisely because they were the conventional and familiar forms of those pronouns (forms used among intimates), and today their only accurate modern equivalents are "you" and "yours." But "thee" and "thou" and "thine" and "thy" have been so long out of everyday use (except in the Society of Friends), that somehow they have become "churchly" sounding, and dignified, perhaps.

We may have already come too far down the road that separates church from life.

An Example: As you can see (if you have read this far), one can go on and on about this subject, so I will conclude by examining only one example of the updating one finds in LW. I should also say that there are a fairly large number of new hymns and new translations, some originating in LBW and others new in LW, which of course by definition escape the "rapacity of the reviser's pen." (nor have I given you updated versions of the examples cited earlier, TLH 394 and TLH 400, though LW updates both of them, because it is not fair to cite only the revised couplet or rime without considering the whole revised version against the whole original version. As in translation, as one learns from experience, if one loses a little in one place, one may gain a little in another place.)

I chose as my example a hymn from the *Worship Supplement* (WS) which is included in an updated version in LW, (CPH, 1982). No question of translation is involved here; the text is English of the 19th century by Walter Chalmers Smith (1824–1908), though the language seems of an earlier vintage. The hymn is notable for its stateliness and dignity, especially in combination with its Welsh tune, and for these qualities I love it dearly, though I would guess that in many Missouri Synod congregations the hymn is unknown.

> Immortal, invisible, God only wise,
> In light inaccessible hid from our eyes,
> Most blessed, most glorious, the Ancient of Days,
> Almighty, victorious, thy great name we praise.
>
> Unresting, unhasting, and silent as light,
> Nor wanting, nor wasting, thou rulest in might;

Thy justice like mountains high soaring above
Thy clouds which are fountains of goodness and love.

To all life thou givest—to both great and small—
In all life thou livest, the true life of all;
We blossom and flourish as leaves on the tree
And wither and perish-but naught changes thee.

Great Father of glory, pure Father of light
Thine angels adore thee, all veiling their sight;
All laud we would render: O help us to see
'Tis only the splendor of light that hides thee.

Problems: The quick eye of the updater immediately sees problems, of course. The "thou" and "thee" and "thy" will have to be changed. This is particularly difficult since "thee" is the riming word of stanza 3, and in both the internal and terminal riming of stanza 4 ("glory/adore thee" and "see/thee"). And the verb endings of stanza 3 ("givest/livest"), also involved in the internal riming, are clearly archaic. The same is true of the contraction "tis" in the last line of stanza 4, and also in the "naught" in the last line of stanza 3. How does the updater "solve" these problems? The following version of the text appears in *Lutheran Worship*, 1982.

Immortal, invisible, God only wise,
In light inaccessible hid from our eyes,
Most blessed, most glorious, O Ancient of Days,
Almighty, victorious, your great name we praise!

Unresting, unhasting, and silent as light,
Not wanting, nor wasting, you rule in your might;
Your justice like mountains high soaring above
Your clouds which are fountains of goodness and love.

All life you engender, in great and in small;
To all life befriender, the true life of all.
We blossom and flourish, in richness and range,
We wither and perish, but you never change.

> Great Father of glory, pure Father of light,
> Your angels adore you, enveiling their sight.
> All laud we would render; oh, lead us to see
> The light of your splendor, your love's majesty!
>
> Copyright © Lutheran Worship, 1982

Pronouns: Some of the updating is quite unexceptional, even routine. One expects simple changes in pronouns on the basis of the bias of the Commission in favor of modern pronouns. One may mourn the loss—"thy great name we praise" may seem more impressive than "your great name we praise"—but what is lost (if it is) in dignity is gained in intimacy, is gained in a more personal relationship. The "rulest" in stanza 2, line 2, is solved simply by the addition of another pronoun, "thou rulest in might" becoming "you rule in your might."

Riming: Stanza three is a much greater problem. Not only are the verb forms "givest/livest" archaic, but they are involved in the internal riming which is the norm of the whole hymn. One might simply insert an emphatic, as in "to all life you give, yes—to both great and small—/in all life you live, yes—the true life of all." The updater here take a greater risk and involves himself in more far-reaching problems. Paraphrasing "To all life thou givest" (note the meaning without the hymnic inversion of word order is "You give life to all"), he hazards "All life you engender." The inversion is still present, yet the possibility of misunderstanding is, to my mind, considerably lessened. The word "engendered" is abstract (a disadvantage) and relatively uncommon (a possible advantage), but consorts agreeably with and echoes words like "immortal, invisible" and "inaccessible" from stanza one.

The consequence of this change, however, of course, is the necessity of finding a riming word for line two which will adequately paraphrase "in all life thou livest." The updater proposes "To all life befriender"; the inversion echoes the previous inversion and here may actually be an aid to immediate understanding. "Befriender" may seem faintly archaic to some, though *The American Heritage Dictionary of the English Language* does not restrictively label "befriend" in any way, and the noun patterning adding-er is ancient and honorable in English. On the positive side, if one's life is befriended by God, it seems to me that the line has gained significantly in emotional warmth.

Combinations: Lines 3 and 4 of stanza 3 also present a major problem in that the riming word in line 4 is the pronoun "thee" ("naught changes thee"). The imagery is effective: "We blossom and flourish as leaves on the tree/And wither and perish—but naught changes thee." ("Changes" in WS sounds in this context like a modern alteration, and one's suspicions are confirmed if one examines the LBW text. Stanza 3, line 4 in LBW uses "changeth" and stanza 4, line 4 uses "hideth." In addition, stanza 4, line 1 in LBW reads "Thou reignest in glory, thou dwellest in light." Without having researched the problem, I would guess the LBW text to be more authentic, and in these details WS already begins an updating process. Hymnologists are noted for tinkering. They changeth anything they think will improve a text for the specific audience they have in mind.) In the updated version the blossoming and flourishing are kept with the riming contrasts in withering and perishing, but "naught changes thee" has the greater power and dignity, though it also has the archaic freight of "naught" and "thee." "You never change," viewed hostilely, may sound like the faint echo of a domestic altercation. Having chosen "change" as the terminal word, the updater is forced to a re-writing of the end of line 3. The "as leaves on the tree" imagery is sacrificed for "We blossom and flourish, in richness and range," which has alliteration to recommend itself for what it loses in concreteness, and one could argue that these new nouns have poetic suggestion in connection with life, and are not out of harmony with the tone of the whole. Another "trick" used by the updater is to introduce the unlikely word first ("range"), which makes the riming word ("change") sound more "right," rather than vice versa.

Coinage?: Finally, there are the alterations in stanza 4. We must hurry on. We note that in lines 1 and 2 the updater is somewhat lame in riming "your glory" with "adore you," although "glory/adore thee," though closer in sound, are not an exact rime in the original either. Line 2 introduces "enveiling," which appears to be the updater's coinage. This may be a completely gratuitous interposition of an unnecessary obstacle. On the other hand, it may be ignored. The meaning, even with the coined word, presents no difficulty. The "thee" rime at the end of the stanza is a more crucial problem, as is the archaic "tis" at the beginning of the line. The updaters solution here is "oh, lead us to see/The light of your splendor, your love's majesty!" In terms of its meaning, "majesty" is a happy choice; unfortunately, the accents of the word fall in somewhat of a disarray. (I have not, to this point, made any issue of how the accents of the text fit the accents of the music; much less the subtler but also telling issue of how the tone of the text matches the tone of the music. The success of the original is adequate evidence.) At any rate, the accents of the word "majesty" fall in the wrong places in relation to the tune, and they supply the only instance in the whole text of a terminal riming word which is not a single, strong, mono-syllabic word. Ah, but the meaning seems so right!

Compromise: Any melding of words to music involves compromises, of course. Whether the compromises of the updater here vitiate the effect of the original by his adherence to his updating principal, or whether the strengthening effect of updating overrides some of the smaller details, is obviously open to argument, and probably will be decided by the taste of the person, who should consider all the nuances of the problem. For myself, I am inclined to award the updater at least a "B." (But then, I know who the updater is, and I can claim no objectivity in this.)

Henry L. Letterman

Original Hymns, Carols, Sacred Texts, and Secular Poems

Abraham's God and Ours

To Abraham's God and ours,
The God of the promise, who gave His name to him,
Calling him to a far country, full of strangers,
Be glory, honor, praise and dominion,
As each new generation faces
The challenge of the Lord's own choosing!

To Israel's God and ours,
The pillar of flame in the trackless wilderness,
He who leads us through large troubles, always faithful,
Whose Spirit forms us pilgrimage people
Let each new generation witness
The wonder of the Lord's leading!

Our father's strong God, and ours,
Our refuge of ages, who made us sons of His,
He whose death on the cross covers our transgression,
And turns our living upward and outward
Let each new generation grasp it:
The rescue of the Lord's redeeming!

In darkness and sin we pray,
For light of Thy coming, for courage, strength, and joy,
God of Abraham, our Father make us worthy
To sing Thy praise with saints and with martyrs,
In white of Thy salvation robe us,
In witness clouds of heaven's glory!

Copyright © Henry L. Lettermann

A Carpenter My Father
A Song of Jesus

A carpenter my Father,
A gentle man is He,
His hammer blows resounding
Not far from Galilee!
He planes His planks of cedar,
He joins them craftily,
His corners clean and fitted so
His work's a joy to see!

My Father's skill in shaping
The knotted wood to hand,
With iron tools for cutting,
And smoothing tools to sand,
Has carved me to his purpose
Upon His lathing stand,
Has turned and shaped His sure design
Exactly as he planned!

The cheerful chips fly upward,
The beam is made to be
The central soul's abutment,
The soaring ceiling free!
The work I do, He saw it,
In what He formed in me,
The house of refuge dearly bought
By way of Calvary!

And you who know my story,
My suff'ring and my pain,
Have seen my Easter rising,
The grave where I have lain,
And let no skeptic Thomas
Obscure the truth so plain,
My Father's love triumphant stands,
The grace within the grain!

My Father's will forever,
My Father's will for me!
The churchly house he builds here
Stands full and fair to see!
The corner stone is certain,
The beam a blooming tree,
The threshold leads into His love,
The door—eternity!

Copyright © Henry L. Lettermann

America the Blest

My country, my country
America the free,
From ocean to ocean,
The land of liberty!

Her forests, her mountains,
Her people's humble pride,
Her great bustling cities,
Her peaceful countryside!

My country, my country,
In all her beauty dressed,
From ocean to ocean,
America the Blest!

Copyright © 1967 Concordia Publishing House

An Angel Came to Mary

An angel came to Mary,
When she was all alone,
To tell of Jesus coming,
To make the Good News known.

An angel came to Joseph,
To warn him in a dream,
To take the child and Mary,
To Egypt's distant scene.

An angel walks beside us,
Today he takes our hand,
And he will surely guide us,
Into a heav'nly land.

Copyright © 1961 Concordia Publishing House

And When the Lord Said

And when the Lord said,
"Let there be light!"
The light was grand to see,
And Bethlehem was born!

And when the Lord said,
"Let rainbows be!"
The Gospel burned the black,
And Bethlehem was born!

And when the Lord said,
"Mary, believe!"
The stable glowed with faith,
And Bethlehem was born!

And when the Lord said,
"You are my child!"
His touch redeemed my heart,
And Bethlehem was born!

Copyright © Henry L. Lettermann

As Moses, Lost in Sinai's Wilderness

As Moses, lost in Sinai's wilderness,
Was led in awe before the burning bush,
So have our fathers walked the holy ground
And stammered out God's thoughts and seen his will:

Refrain: God of our fathers,
 God of love,
 Remember us still!

As priests across the surging Jordan bore
With trembling hands the Ark of Covenant,
So have our fathers walked, by you compelled,
The way of sorrows to the sacred hill:

Refrain

As Solomon with gold and cedar wood
Was bold to make your house with human hands,
So have our fathers built these walls in faith,
Your name upon each lintel, sash, and sill:

Refrain

As in the vision of the miracle
Our fathers ventured far in Jesus' name,
So touch the hearts that rise to you in praise,
And let the song of faith your temple fill:

Refrain

Copyright © 1982 Concordia Publishing House

A Strangely Quiet Bethlehem

A strangely quiet Bethlehem
Lies muted in the dust,
No shepherds rouse the silent streets,
No wise men seek with trust!
Today no burst of heav'nly light
Turns darkness into day.
No Mary with a simple heart
Wraps God amidst the hay!

No peace on earth the heralds hymn,
No star to brightly shine.
No Joseph kneeling mute adores
The Savior Son Divine!
Lord, touch this tinsel dying heart,
That darkly yearns Thy birth!
Lord, send Thy gentle warming light
To kindle ancient earth!

Renew again the womb of time,
Create the stable bare,
That all may see Thy shepherding
And know Thy loving care!
Then may the angels leap with joy,
And magi richly give.
Then may the quiet Bethlehem
Awake and sing and live!

Copyright © Henry L. Lettermann

At Evening

Now has the weary sun slipped
    down to the sky,
Earth now is sleeping,
    and so soon shall I.

Father, I thank thee
    that during this day
Thy hand has led me in work
    and in play.

Father, forgive me the wrongs
    I have done,
Bless those I love and, Lord,
    bless everyone.

Then in Thy love I will rest
    through this night;
Lead, Lord, through the darkness and
    bring me to light.

Copyright © 1965 Concordia Publishing House

A White Lily Blows

When Christ comes to die on Calvary
Created things all hold their breath;
They hide their face in the darkened sky,
And nothing moves on that hillside except –
A white lily blows, blows,
A white lily blows in the dark heart of spring!

When Mary in doubt that Easter dawn
Believes her Lord among the dead,
She weeps her shuddering grief against
The stubborn stone in the garden and there –
A white lily blows, blows,
A white lily blows in the dark heart of spring!

When death with its terror comes by night
Disquieting my solitude
My Christ who arose from the dead proclaims
The empty grave in the garden and then –
A white lily blows, blows,
A white lily blows in the dark heart of spring!

Copyright © Henry L. Lettermann

Best You Sleep Now, Little Jesus

Best you sleep now, little Jesus,
Best you sleep now, little child,
In the morning I see Herod's soldiers,
Looking sharp for Jesus Child.
Trouble find you fast and early,
Best you sleep now, Jesus Child!

Best you sleep now, little Jesus,
Best you sleep now little child,
In the morning I see crowds to jeer you,
Down the road to Egypt land.
Trouble find you fast and early,
Best you sleep now, Jesus Child!

Best you sleep now, little Jesus,
Best you sleep now, little child,
In the morning I see Calvary's suffering,
Thorns to wear for Jesus child.
Trouble find you fast and early,
Best you sleep now, Jesus child!

Best you sleep now, little Jesus,
Best you sleep now, little child,
In the morning in your Father's blessing,
Golden crowns for Jesus Child.
No more trouble ever find you,
You can sleep now, Jesus Child!

Copyright © Henry L. Lettermann

Birthday Greeting

A happy birthday wish
We pray for you today,
That Jesus keep you safe from harm,
And never let you stray.

For He will take you in His arms
And drive away your fear,
And hold you in his love until
Your birthday comes next year.

Copyright © 1961 Concordia Publishing House

Caught in the Storm of Earth's Uncertain Life

Caught in the storm of earth's uncertain life,
Taken and tossed by diverse winds contrary,
Seeking to touch you, Lord, within the cloud,
Trusting somehow your covenant eternal,
    Tremb'ling we come before your throne
    Willful and wayward creatures,
    Sons who have strayed so far from home,
    We, who resist your leading –
Re-form our hearts with your salvation!

Mankind in ruin seeks its selfish way,
Here where injustice always seems to triumph,
Where hate is strong and ego rampant rules,
Here stands your church, divided and dividing –
    Shape us, your instruments of clay,
    Reclaim your lost creation,
    Send us with reconciling grace,
    Forgiven and forgiving –
Lord, hear our earnest supplication!

Teach us the words that heal the broken heart,
Touch us with love when we touch one another,
Make straight the way for Christ within the gloom,
Christ, who proclaims resistless revolution –
    O, let the boldness of our acts,
    Reach out with promise blessing,
    Reckless of cost like Christ himself,
    In serving, loving, healing –
Lord, give us your own consecration!

Not with the strength of human hands we work,
But with our Father's re-creative guiding,
Not by ourselves will love enflame the earth,
But by our Savior's suffering and dying,
    Lord, with your spirit stir our hearts,
    Your miracles sustain us
    Your hand, supportless, raise us up,
    To highest heaven's portals –
In us live out your exaltation!

Copyright © Henry L. Lettermann

Chickadee

Up the mountain where the steeple stabs the sky,
In the snow where fresh-dug earth is piled so high,
Chickadee, how can you sing so cheerfully?
Now he's gone, and spring will never come for me.

Copyright © 1967 Concordia Publishing House

Christ Our King

The wise men awed are worshipping
Before the starlit gift to earth;
We with them kneel and tribute bring,
And pay our homage to His birth!
Let all forgiven mankind sing,
The gracious reign of Christ our King!

Let Herod and let Caesar rage,
Beneath the Lord's compelling hands;
All that the prophets did presage,
In Jesus' birth completed stands!
No more shall death's despairing wage,
The stricken souls of men engage!

The holy seraphim take wing,
Before His throne triumphantly;
Almighty Infant conquering,
We celebrate Thy victory!
Let all redeemed creation sing,
The glorious reign of Christ our King!

Copyright © Henry L. Lettermann

Continually Triumphant Seraphim

Continually triumphant seraphim,
That countless throng before Thy brilliant throne,
With all created things Thy glory hymn!
We name Thee Lord,
Thou who art God alone!

Before Thy throne the martyr lays his sword,
Apostles, prophets see Thee face to face,
In Thee the faithful know their great reward!
We name Thee Lord,
Thou who art God alone!

The Father who forgives and justifies,
Who washed us in His Spirit's holy fire,
The Son who died our willing sacrifice!
We name Thee Lord,
Thou who art God alone!

Though here we struggle in a dark'ning land,
That sees no more Thy face nor finds Thy way,
Let faith outspoken and unshaken stand!
We name Thee Lord,
Thou who art God alone!

Thy church expectant, Lord in penitence,
In labor and in longing hope awaits,
Thy promise coming, our deliverance!
We name Thee Lord,
Thou who art God alone!

Copyright © Henry L. Lettermann

Dear Father, Lord of All

Dear Father, Lord of all
    To your high throne we come;
    Our backward thoughts recall,
    Let not our lips be dumb:
To you we sing
    For years of grace within this place
    Our thanks we bring.

The sins that you forgave
    Remain forgiven yet;
    The hearts you came to save
    Your love cannot forget!
Oh Savior dear,
    You, on your cross, Redeemed our loss
    Your love is here.

Here are the washing streams
    Where children find your face;
    And here the pulpit gleams
    of your free-given grace!
Your Spirit's might
    In bread and wine, Your altar's sign
    Sustains our light.

A city on the hill
    God's truth to emphasize,
    His holy cross yet will
    lift high before men's eyes!
Your loving name
    O father, Son, in Spirit one,
    We here proclaim.

Copyright © Henry L. Lettermann

I Am Jesus' Letter

I am Jesus' letter,
Sent to all my friends,
Showing them with actions,
What the Lord intends.

Telling them that Jesus
Died the world to win,
Telling them to love Him
Who forgives their sin.

Let me be a message,
Drawn in letters plain,
Let me tell the story,
Of the Savior slain.

Let me say to each one,
Come to Jesus side,
Hold to Him forever,
In His love abide.

Copyright © 1961 Concordia Publishing House

Injun Summer

When Injun summer walks the land
An' leaves turn red and yeller,
Old homesick injun ghosts return,
All hazy like and meller!

Them injuns dance and smoke their pipes,
And when we folks get sleepy,
A million spirits red, like leaves,
Dance round them corn-shock teepees!

Copyright © 1967 Concordia Publishing House

Editor's note: Although the language and sentiment expressed in this poem are regrettable by today's standards, we felt it was important to include this text so that the entire body of Dr. Lettermann's work might be found in one volume.

In Little Bethlehem

In little Bethlehem
The Savior comes again;
The eastern star drops down from heaven above!
Behind a stable door,
Within a manger poor,
Begins the reign of Jesus, Lord of Love!

Without a major stir
The miracle occurs;
The eastern star drops down from heaven above!
Here in a tiny form,
Here in a baby born,
Begins the reign of Jesus, Lord of love!

And wise men stop, wide eyed,
To search the secret skies;
The eastern star drops down from heaven above!
A simple shepherd's faith
Awakens the world to truth,
Begins the reign of Jesus, Lord of love!

In little Bethlehem
The Savior comes again;
The eastern star drops down from heaven above!
Behind a stable door
Within a manger poor,
Begins the reign of Jesus, Lord of love!

Copyright © Henry L. Lettermann

In the Morning

In the morning, bright-eyed morning,
In the morning dawns the sun,
In the evening, gray-haired evening,
In the evening shadows run.

In the morning, bright-eyed morning,
In the morning work to do,
In the evening, gray-haired evening,
In the evening work is through.

In the morning, bright-eyed morning,
In the morning trust God's grace,
In the evening, gray-haired evening,
In the evening touch His face.

In the morning, bright-eyed morning,
In the morning dawns the sun,
In the evening, gray-haired evening,
In the evening day is done.

Copyright © 1967 Concordia Publishing House

In the Winter

In the winter snowflakes fall,
Crystal ices house and hall,
In the winter whiteness is all!

In the winter snowflakes fall,
Pine and spruce grow Christmas tall,
In the winter God's gift is all!

Copyright © 1967 Concordia Publishing House

I Wonder, I Wonder

I wonder, I wonder why sunsets are red,
And I wonder why skies look so blue,
I wish I could know, it wonders me so!

Oh, I wonder, I wonder how clouds carry rain,
And I wonder why thunder's so loud,
I wish I could know, it wonders me so!

I wonder, I wonder how trees grow so tall,
And I wonder why things get so green,
I wish I could know, it wonders me so!

I wonder, I wonder why God loves me so,
And I wonder how Jesus could die,
I wish I could know, it wonders me so!

Copyright © 1966 Concordia Publishing House

Lead Us, Lord

Lost, wandering like Israel's children,
We came at last to this chosen land,
And found it good, beyond deserving,
Full of the milk and honey of his love!
Lead us, Lord, fulfill in us your holy will!

We, too had seen the Red Sea's parting,
Had known our Lord in fearful Sinai's law,
Had drunk at bitter Marah's welling,
Eaten his manna every morning new!
Lead us, Lord, fulfill in us your holy will!

Still blessing this resplendent wasteland
With us the loving Lord makes covenant:
Forgiveness free without condition,
Purchased in bread and blood by Jesus Christ!
Lead us, Lord, fulfill in us your holy will!

This promised land reveals his goodness,
The lonely axes sound in wilderness
Becomes the harvest's rich out-pouring,
City and farm convulsed in equity!
Lead us, Lord, fulfill in us your holy will!

God save this land of mis-redemption,
Where Christ is born in sinful hearts again,
America, it's freedom flying,
Find in God's love his bold transforming power!
Lead us, Lord, fulfill in us your holy will!

Copyright © Henry L. Lettermann

Like Sea and Air and Sky

Like sea and air and sky,
The faithful Christian teacher
Cares naught for seasons;
The teacher shines on bidden like the stars,
and asks no reasons.

He speaks the Christ he knows
From intimate acquaintance,
From hardy living
Like sunshine after rain, He bursts with bloom
His witness giving.

In cold, dark, hopeless times,
He leads his wand'ring people
With light unswerving,
His patient, caring love surround us here
Beyond deserving.

Like sea and air and sky,
The faithful Christian teacher
cares naught for the seasons;
The teacher shines on bidden like the stars,
And asks no reasons.

Copyright © Henry L. Lettermann

Lord, Bless the Manger-Child

When Jesus comes to Bethlehem
So secret silently,
The midnight glows with light of dawn
In quiet mystery!
Lord, bless the manger-child,
And. Lord, bless me!

When shepherds in the dewy hills
Hear angels in the sky,
They sing the shout that has no words
For God's own lullaby!
Lord, bless the manger-child,
And, Lord, bless me!

When wisemen from the east appear
To give the gifts of praise,
Their rich perfume of poverty
His humble wealth displays!
Lord, bless the manger-child,
And, Lord, bless me!

When darkling shadows touch the child,
Then we with Mary see
The bitter thorns and crowing cross
Of joyous Calvary!
Lord, bless the manger-child,
And, Lord, bless me!

Copyright © 1976 Concordia Publishing House

Lord God, Reform Our Hearts

Institutions ordered by man
Cannot, for their human ways,
Contain God's great mysterious working of good:
Alleluia! Lord God, reform our hearts!

The disarming grace of the Lord,
In Calvary's ransom tree,
Has bought a new unworthy mankind with love:
Alleluia! Lord God, reform our hearts!

The persistent spirit of God
Pursues ev'ry orphan soul,
And in the family of faith gives his peace:
Alleluia! Lord, God, reform our hearts!

And the church of God's own design
Proclaims in its war of love
That it shall burst down heaven's door
With His praise:
Alleluia! Lord God, reform our hearts!

Copyright © Henry L. Lettermann

Lord Jesus Christ, the Children's Friend

Lord Jesus Christ, the children's friend,
To each of them your presence send;
Call them by name and keep them true
In loving faith, dear Lord, to you.

In Christian homes, Lord, let them be
Your blessing to their family;
Let Christian schools your work extend
In living truth as you intend.

That caring parents, gracious Lord,
And faithful teachers find reward
In leading these, to whom you call,
To find in Christ their all in all.

For by your word we clearly see
That we have sinned continually;
But show us too, forgiving Lord,
Your saving Gospel's great reward.

That all of us, your children dear,
By Christ redeemed, may Christ revere;
Lead us in joy that all we do
Will witness to our love for you.

Then guard and keep us to the end,
Secure in you, our gracious friend,
That in your heav'nly family
We sing your praise eternally.

Copyright © 1982 Concordia Publishing House

Morning Round

Breezes blow, roosters crow,
Let sleepy dawn break,
Good morning, good morning,
God's earth is wide awake!

Copyright © 1967 Concordia Publishing House

Mount Rushmore, USA

From the Black Hill's storied mountain
Springs the sculptor's dream of grandeur,
High above the Great Plains towering,
Proud America's memorial!

Stately Washington, our father,
Jefferson, who penned our freedom,
Lincoln wrapped in solemn greatness,
Roosevelt, the rough and ready!

From the Black Hill's storied mountain
Springs the sculptor's dream of grandeur,
High above the Great Plains towering,
Proud America's memorial!

Copyright © 1967 Concordia Publishing House

Northwest Passage

Out from Bristol and Amsterdam,
Bold buccaneers with only one thought
Find the passage to wealth untold,
Follow the vision gold begot!

Refrain: Westward ho, hearties,
Bound for the setting sun, look away,
Westward ho, hearties,
Bound for the riches of Cathay!

Hudson, Cabot, and Frobisher,
Eager the hearts, the hands rough but strong,
Through America lay the way,
Bold buccaneers with but one song!

Refrain: Westward ho, hearties,
Bound for the setting sun, look away,
Westward ho, hearties,
Bound for the riches of Cathay!

Copyright © 1967 Concordia Publishing House

Not with the Strength

Not with the strength of hands
Build we Jerusalem's wall,
Nor could our human craft avoid
The fate of Jericho's fall,
But by Thy grace, Lord God of hosts,
All that is not of Thee is none of ours!

Copyright © Henry L. Lettermann

Old Man Mississippi

From Lake Itasca's icy stream,
By mossy rocks and ledges,
Through limpid pools where game fish gleam
Begins the Mississippi!

Through villages where crossroads meet
And under countless bridges,
Past farmer's fields of corn and wheat
Meanders Mississippi!

Pursued by road and railroad track,
Through busy towns and cities,
With steamboat cargo on its back
Flows mighty Mississippi!

With gath'ring force the torrent roars,
Through New Orleans and farther
Down to the gulf its tribute pours
The rushing Mississippi!

So tell the tale and sing the song
Of nature's shining wonder;
The nation's heart is swept along
By Old Man Mississippi!

Copyright © 1967 Concordia Publishing House

On Christmas Morning Children Sing

Refrain: On Christmas morning children sing,
            Here in the manger lies our king:
            From loving hearts his praises spring.
            On Christmas morning we greet our King!

Large and small, children all,
Join in the song that has no end;
Earth and sky,
All reply,
Jesus has come to be our friend!

Refrain

Christmas tree, Calvary,
Crossing in God's most awesome plan;
Sin and grace,
Face to face,
Bringing together God and man!

Refrain

Oh, my Lord, here adored,
Find in my song your answered call;
Sin and grace,
Face to face,
Jesus, redeeming mankind's fall!

Refrain

Copyright © 1983 Concordia Publishing House

On Galilee's High Mountain

On Galilee's high mountain
Christ gave the great command
In words of strength and promise
Which all can understand:
"All power to me is given
To do what I shall choose;
Therefore I send my children,
Their witness I shall use."

The Lord, who born of Mary,
Came down as man and died,
Who preached to all who listened,
For us was crucified
This Lord, our living brother,
In pow'r at God's right hand,
Has chosen us to carry
His truth to every land.

His strength within my weakness
Will make me bold to say
How his redeeming power
Transforms my stubborn clay;
His touch of fire ignites me,
With courage I am sent,
My tongue tied silence broken,
With grace made eloquent.

And not alone to nations
In far away retreats,
But everywhere I broadcast
His love through crowded streets:
The lives that my life touches,
However great or small
Let them through me see Jesus,
Who served and saved us all.

That everyone he chooses,
For reasons of his own,
Will find in Christ his calling
To live his love alone.
His presence always leads us
Till time shall no more be;
Christ's strength, his love, his comfort
Gives us his victory.

Lord, gather all your children,
Wherever they may be,
And lead them on to heaven
To live eternally
With you, our loving Father,
And Christ, Our brother dear,
Whose Spirit guards and gives us
The joy to persevere.

Copyright © 1982 Concordia Publishing House

Our Father, Who from Heaven Above

Our Father, who from heav'n above
Has turned toward us the face of love,
Bless us, your children, with your name;
Its holy wonders now proclaim;
Your kingdom and your will alone
Through us and in us here make known.

Give us this day our daily bread
As ev'ry life by you is fed;
Forgive our sins' enormities
As we forgive our enemies;
Let no temptation us betray
Nor evil threaten us, we pray.

Yours is the kingdom, yours alone
The constant praise before your throne;
All pow'rs and all dominions, Lord,
Are subject to your mighty word;
All glory yours, by ev'ry tongue
Forever let your praise be sung!

Copyright © 1982 Concordia Publishing House

Our Savior Kindly Calls

Our Savior kindly calls
His children to His breast,
To give us pardon for our sins,
To give us peace and rest.

With water and the Word
Our Savior made us His,
Invited us to be His own,
To be baptized and live.

His arms are open wide
His children to receive,
To bless us with His healing hand,
To teach us to believe.

Copyright © 1961 Concordia Publishing House

Prayer

Morning, evening, noon, and night,
For all Thy gifts we thank Thee, Lord.

Copyright © 1967 Concordia Publishing House

St. Luke: The Gentile Stranger

In far off Syrian Antioch
The Gentile stranger heard Thy call
And laid before the crucified
His heart, his learning, and his all!

Physician to the mighty Paul,
With gentle, willing hands he came
To heal the hurt in hearts forlorn,
To launch the spirit's bruising flame!

To write the story of the Christ
With scientific eye and mind,
And in the record of his grace
The poetry of God-head find!

May we with equal diligence,
Whatever be our time or place,
Rededicate ourselves to Thee,
In each perceive our Father's face!

For all Thy saints we praise the name,
The proof of Thy forgiving Word,
Make us Thy witnesses as they,
Then we Thy children, Thou our Lord!

Copyright © 1968 Concordia Publishing House

Softly, Softly, Sleep Jesus

Softly, softly, sleep Jesus
Peacefully rest in Thy cradle of straw.
Softly, softly, sleep Jesus
Silent in wonder we worship Thee.

Soon enough Herod would take Thee to smite Thee
Soon enough suff'ring would claim Thee her own.

Softly, softly, sleep Jesus
Peacefully rest in Thy cradle of straw.
Softly, softly, sleep Jesus
Here Thou shalt find Thee a shelter from might.

Copyright © Henry L. Lettermann

Song of the Liberty Bell

Ding, dong, ding, dong
Loud and long!

Ring out freedom, joy prolong, for
Wild and sweet is freedom's song!

Ring out ecstatic the joy our proclaiming, the
Wild exaltation of liberty's song!

Copyright © 1967 Concordia Publishing House

So Shall Our Song of Praise

So shall our song of praise burst from
The prison of the earth.
Sweep away the stars,
Swell the chorus of the martyrs,
    saints, and of the Holy Seraphim.

Cry out and shout
    for great is he who dwells with us.
Cry out and shout
    for great is our God.

Copyright © Henry L. Lettermann

Spring Is Springing

Spring is springing, oh, what a day!
Flowers are flow'ring, spring, hooray!

Leaves are leaving, oh, what a day!
Children are singing, spring, hooray!

Copyright © 1967 Concordia Publishing House

Still Are the Hills

Still are the hills over Bethlehem town,
Even sheepfolds are hushed now, the flocks bedded down;
The shepherds alone in that dark starry night
Are watching and waiting for the coming of light.

Suddenly angels, announcing His birth,
With the bright song of heaven illumine the earth,
Hosanna, hosanna, all warfare must cease,
God's gift of the Savior has declared us at peace.

Gladly the shepherds their footsteps they haste
To the stable to gaze on God's small human face,
And gladly proclaim it in accents of awe,
The great God Messiah lies asleep in the straw.

Those who receive Him, how blessed are they,
To be filled with the wonder of God's own birthday,
He gives us Himself here, what miracle this,
His coming how gentle to the heart that is His!

Copyright © 1973 Concordia Publishing House

Still, Still, Wind and Will

Still, still, wind and will be still, be still.
Softly let us listen to the sad symphonic whisper
Of the falling leaves.
Still, still, wind and will be still, be still.

Copyright © Henry L. Lettermann

That We Might Believe
A text for a cantata

I.

Narrative:
Black, black, black is the stain
of that incredible Friday
when the created creature kills the creator.

Chorus:
We find our face
in that faceless crowd,
with catcalls we jeered him,
with the nails of everyday
we crucify him.

Dialogue:
    One: Will these bones live?
    Two: The Lord is dead.
    One: The Lord, quick and mighty —
    Two: is dead in the earth.
        in the midnight of despair
        death only is the Lord of all.

II.

Narrative:
Three weak women then
and two disciples
dumbfounded realize the dawn
of a perpetual miracle.
He is risen indeed!

Chorus:
Sin that held us captive
is our prisoner,
Death that was our tyrant
is our slave,

and out of agony
The whole world stirs, awakes.

Dialogue:
>One: Did he die for me?
>Two: For all mankind.
>One: And did he rise?
>Two: Once, forever.
>One: Does he live?
>Two: Go into Gallilee and see.

III.

Narrative:
Forty days the Lord
broke the bread with them, ate fish,
speaking the mysteries of the kingdom,
and above a small hill
a small cloud hid him,
and he ate no more with them.

Chorus:
The world crowds around us,
Thick and fast and darkness threatens,
Will we forget his rising?
As those born out of time,
oh Lord, appear to us.

Dialogue:
>One: Then he is Lord of all?
>Two: At the right hand with the power.
>One: But does he walk upon the earth?
>Two: He himself, but also with your feet.
>One: And does he heal the sick in spirit?
>Two: By his word and work
>>and with your hands and voices
>>his wonder is revealed.

IV.

Narrative:
Into the unsuspecting world
with mighty sound of rushing wind
the Lord unleashed the fire.

Chorus:
Wash us in thy fire,
sear us with thy mark,
fill us with thy love
that we may conquer worlds,
devour nations, teach
unnumbered multitudes
the glory of thy coming.

For all these things are done
that we might believe,
and believing,
we will die
and find life.

Copyright © Henry L. Lettermann

The Black of Night in Bethlehem

The black of night in Bethlehem
Is lighted up by a star.
In secret, silence stillness comes
The Son of God from far
To where His parents are!

The dawn glows red in Bethlehem
Upon a northern hill.
Within his palace Herod stirs,
Against the morning chill,
To work his wily will!

The innocents of Bethlehem
Are mercilessly slain,
And weeping fills the valley where
The cold white snow has lain
Upon the guiltless plain!

In Egypt green the growing child,
In full obedience,
Prepares to change the blackened earth
To red of penitence
And white of innocence!

Copyright © Henry L. Lettermann

The Children of the Faith

The children of the faith
Walk softly on to God,
With bold, mysterious feet they tread
The path their fathers trod,
While all around them rage,
Wildly without relief,
Attacking foes and doubting hearts,
Storm clouds of unbelief!

The children of the faith
Alive courageously
Have seen the costly love that died
For them on Calvary!
Baptized, confirmed, confessed,
Upward to God's designed,
And taught by father's failing hands,
God-Father's grace they find!

The children of the faith
The lightning in the gloom,
Ignite the sullen tree of earth,
With ransom fire consume,
And after pierce with light,
Earth, by the Spirit's sword,
For children of the living faith
Witness the living Lord!

Copyright © Henry L. Lettermann

The Christ-Child King

The Christ-Child king sleeps in his cradle;
Our muddled world pauses,
Dumbfounded by this heavenly sign.

In the cold of winter
In the palace of ice,
The thaw begins with the sun,
God's Son, the sacrifice.

Still the heat of his love
And the light of the star
Begin to burn in the dark
Like signals from afar.

As the slow sky lightens,
Hope begins to revive;
God's Christmas-justice is born,
His spirit comes alive.

The Christ-Child king sleeps in his cradle;
Our muddled world pauses,
Dumbfounded by this heavenly sign.

Copyright © 1986 Augsburg Publishing House

The Great Puddles

When a little raindrop comes running down the sky,
It becomes a puddle before you blink your eye!

Puddles soon turn into pond and lake,
Little lakes grow big for wetness sake!

Michigan, Ontario, my, how the puddles grew,
Erie and Superior, and even Huron too!

Copyright © 1967 Concordia Publishing House

The Judas Tree
A Cantata

I.

the earth is full of ancient bloom
as the flaming judas tree
greets the spring with glory,
the earth is satiate with
the fragrance of the pale pink blossoms

but it is not hope
that lifts slender fingers
among the branches,
but the old irredeemable wrong,
the faint hearty smell of dung
in the evening air
that has made the ground
unnaturally barren

what thou doest
do quickly

II.

the judas tree darkens
against the evening sky

like a cancer of hideous growth
bursting out of the dank ground
like a poison tree in the wind
scattering black metallic petals,
thirty indelible silver betrayals
jangle and clank in my soul,
I am engulfed with their roaring

Hail master

III.

a little while
in the earth's bosom
is it hard to die?
(to be born again is to die first)
no, no,
it is too difficult
to walk every day with death
to lie down at night with a shroud,
but I have kissed, no the master,
I have taken guilt to mistress
and have begotten estrangement

See thou to that

IV.

Then let me hang myself
upon the tree of Judas
an adulterer of God,
I am drunken, forgetful,
with ancient despair
the flung silver tinkles derisive
against heaven's
iron door:
curse God and die

the potter's field
to bury strangers in

V.

then having died
be re-born

for faint as the reticence of light
in the shy spring morning
touching tenderly the lips of Judas

for surely as the pink arms spread
to call the earth to bring forth prodigies
So imperceptibly,
under that other tree across the Chedron
the stranger child is born a son,
the burden of decay in the earth
blossoms with mystery into song

old pink hands, strangely mine,
clutch the newborn bloom
my christening dress of glory.

Copyright © Henry L. Lettermann

The Lord Be Your Shepherd

The Lord be your shepherd,
The Lord be your guide,
In ev'ry day's endeavor
His love be at your side,
The Lord will guard and keep you,
His goodness will provide.

If trouble or danger,
If sickness betide,
If friends should prove unfaithful,
Or death with you abide,
The Lord will guard and keep you,
His goodness will provide.

The Lord be your shepherd,
The Lord be your guide,
In ev'ry day's endeavor
His love be at your side,
The Lord will guard and keep you,
His goodness will provide.

Copyright © 1966 Concordia Publishing House

The Lord Is My Light

My enemies gather and surround me, mocking my Lord:
Now show us indeed that He helps you!
Their words assail me, venomous slander against my Lord,
He who gave them life!
My Father is He who framed the heavens,
Lord evermore;
His love is sufficient for my life.

And only one thing have I beseeched Him: that I may live
forever and ever in His heart.
His love enthralls me; each day more richly
His name is spelled out among the stars.
I give Him my life, shout my conviction,
Him I adore!
No man can confound this rock of faith!

Give glory to God, our gracious Father, Lord evermore,
for He is the stronghold of our lives.
Give praise to Jesus, our Servant Savior,
for He was raised high upon the tree.
His Spirit enflames us by His witness,
filling our hearts.
Our stronghold, Jehovah, cannot fail!

Copyright © 1971 Concordia Publishing House

The Lord's My Shepherd, Leading Me

The Lord's my shepherd, leading me
To pastures newly green;
Deep flow the waters of his care,
His mercies unforeseen.
He loves me so, he leads me to
His pastures newly green.

My hungry soul he fills again
With manna from above;
He sets my footsteps right again
In pathways of his love.
For his name's sake he nurtures me
With manna from above.

Even within the vale of death
I feel no threat'ning chill,
His rod and staff protecting me,
His love beside me still.
His guardian love protecting me,
I feel no threat of ill.

How he confounds my enemies
By richly blessing me;
His cup of promise overflows
With generosity.
Anointing me his chosen one,
He richly blesses me.

I take my stand forevermore
within my shepherd's fold,
Secure in his forgiving love.
How gently strong his hold!
He loves me so, he leads me to
His blessings rich and bold.

Copyright © 1981 Henry L. Lettermann

The Name of Jesus Sweetly Sounds

The name of Jesus sweetly sounds
To Simeon's anxious ear.
Is this the long-awaited Christ,
This baby crying here?

He takes the child into his hands
Among the temple stones,
He calls for Anna, prophetess,
In earnest joyful tones.

He lifts the child, to offer him,
And knows that God above
Accepts the Child who sets us free,
Who manifests his love!

So Simeon sings his song of death,
As even so shall we,
Who rest assured in Jesus' cross
Redeemed eternally!

And Jesus' name still sweetly sounds,
And Jesus hears our praise,
The Son who shows his Father's love
Until the end of days!

Copyright © Henry L. Lettermann

The Precious Gift

The world in sin was fast asleep.
The darkness covered all.
The voice of Joseph in the street
Re-echoed from a wall,
Re-echoed from a wall.

With weary heart the virgin bore
A mother's anxious quest.
In doubt God's parents stood before
The world's door seeking rest,
The world's door seeking rest.

In mystery the Father sends
The precious gift of light.
His son, our substitute, descends,
Redeems us from the night,
Redeems us from the night.

He lies in dusty stable then,
In manger of the ox;
He comes into the hearts of men,
Announced to humble flocks,
Announced to humble flocks.

Copyright © Henry L. Lettermann

The Wind of the Sea

The wind of the sea finds the welcoming land,
It climbs the steep mountains with showery ease,
Blow, blow, wind of the sea,
And tumble down leeward, with searching blast!

Then sweep through the plains,
    bearing snow cloud and storm,
And kiss the great lakes and the shy eastern hills,
Blow, blow, wind of the sea,
Oh, blow through my country, the land that I love!

Copyright © 1967 Concordia Publishing House

This Is the Cross of Christ

And did God's feet in times before
Bruise the Judean stones?
And did He walk with thirsting heart
This desert of dry bones?

Refrain:
This is the cross of Christ, the Son,
who with the Father makes us one!

Are these the hands that healed the sick
Touched them with cooling grace?
These gnarled hands that grasped the nails
That put Him in my place?

Refrain

Men pierced His side in vengeful glee,
Water and blood I see;
But life and death on Calvary's tree
His spirit teaches me!

Refrain

I walk the world with zealous heart,
Eager my hands to act!
My feet His feet, His heart my heart,
His love my only fact!

Refrain

Copyright © Henry L. Lettermann

Watchmen on the Wall of Zion

Watchmen on the wall of Zion,
What's the watchword, can you tell?
Though the darkness seems to gather,
All is well, all is well.
Though the darkness seems to gather,
All is well.

Will the bridegroom soon be coming,
Soon arriving, can you tell?
He is waiting at your threshold,
Hear the bell, hear the bell!
He is waiting at your threshold,
Hear the bell!

Will his advent change our lifestyle,
Turn us back from sin's black hell?
You are now his new creation,
I can tell, I can tell!
You are now his new creation,
I can tell!

Then he died indeed to free us
From the curse of sin's dread spell?
You are born to resurrection,
Hear the bell, hear the bell!
You are born to resurrection,
Hear the bell!

Watchman on the wall of Zion,
Let us be his citadel!
Rocked in his redeeming cradle,
All is well, all is well!
Rocked in his redeeming cradle,
All is well!

Copyright © Henry L. Lettermann

What News This Bitter Night

What news, what news this bitter night
When all is sheltered in the gloom?
No news except a baby born,
Who finds within an ox's stall
His narrow room!

What men are these that hurry past?
What wonder do they run to see?
Shepherds who heard the herald's song,
Who haste in stable to adore
The mystery!

What child is this, who sleeping makes
The manger throne His resting place?
None but the king of heaven high,
Born into dying to redeem
Our fallen race!

What shall I bring to honor Him,
What homage pay, what poor gift give?
Naught but your heart which, dead in sin,
Finds in this child forgiving love
And strength to live!

Copyright © Henry L. Lettermann

When Time Is Full, the Stars Ignite

When time is full, the stars ignite,
Prophets their scrolls rehearse,
Isaiah's pain and Micah's curse
And ancient Eden's curse –
Clairvoyant ages wait
The coming of the infant Christ
To claim His king's estate!

The dust of time cannot bedim
Simeon's sighted eyes,
Nor aged Anna's hope in Him,
Nor Mary's trust revise –
With confidence they wait
The coming of the infant Christ
To claim His king's estate!

So, through the back streets of the mind,
Rumored the faith takes form,
The shock of grace for humankind,
The stillness in the storm –
In hope the ages wait
The coming of the infant Christ
To claim His king's estate!

And timeless down eternal years
Christ, in His living, dies;
And fixed within time's curse appears
God's love, His great surprise!
The wondering ages wait
The coming of the infant Christ
To claim His king's estate!

Copyright © Henry L. Lettermann

Who Are These That Earnest Knock

Who are these that earnest knock,
Seeking some safe haven,
These in lonely streets that walk,
Weak and heavy laden?
Joseph and the virgin mild
Seeking shelter for the child
Yet unborn but near;
Let me ready room for Him,
I will take the Christ child in,
Humbly pay Him welcome.

Who is this that docile lies
In a lowly cradle?
Who is this that dignifies
This rude, common stable?
Christ, the ever-living Lord,
By the angel hosts adored,
Come to meet His death.
O Redeemer of my sin,
Oh, how great Thy love has been
To be born to save me.

Who are these that silent stand,
Filled with holy wonder,
Proselyte and pilgrim band,
Thousand without number?
Shepherds, sages, saints whose eyes
See the newborn Sacrifice
With discerning faith.
All unworthy, yet make me
One who sees in majesty,
One who kneels adoring.

Copyright © 1969 Concordia Publishing House

Who Found America

Who was the first explorer,
Who found America?
Ev'ryone says Columbus,
In one four nine and two.
Isn't it queer,
Nothing is clear,
No one really is sure?
Whose was the bold heart seeking
The dark and uncertain shore?

Who was the first explorer,
Who found America?
Was it perhaps John Cabot,
First on the continent?
Some say the Norse came first, of course.
When did the Indians come?
Whose was the bold heart seeking,
Who really was the first to come?

Copyright © 1967 Concordia Publishing House

With Flame of Might

With flame of might Saint Michael goes
God's holy war to wage,
And we who follow seize the sword,
With martyr, saint and sage!

Refrain:
Alleluia, angels above and risen saints
Praise your glorious name, alleluia!

On battle ground terrestrial
We march with spirits light
Surrounded by a guardian host,
Arrayed in heavenly white!

Refrain

Around your throne celestial
The living, dying, dead,
Are gathered in the blessed throng
With Christ, our heart, our head!

Refrain

Copyright © 1966 Concordia Publishing House

Translations of German Hymns

A Lamb Alone Bears Willingly

A lamb alone bears willingly
Sin's crushing weight for sinners;
He carries guilt's enormity,
Dies shorn of all his honors.
He goes to slaughter, weak and faint,
Is led away with no complaint
His spotless life to offer.
He bears the stripes, the wrath, the lies,
The mockery, and yet replies,
"Willing all this I suffer."

This lamb is Christ, our soul's great friend,
The Lamb of God, our Savior,
Whom God the Father chose to send
Our rebel guilt to cover.
"Go down, my Son," the Father said,
"To free my children from their dread
Of death and condemnation.
The wrath and stripes are hard to bear,
But in your death they all can share
The joy of your salvation!"

"Yes, Father, yes, most willingly
I bear what you command me;
My will conforms to your decree,
I risk what you have asked me."
O wondrous love, what have you done?
The Father offers up his Son,
The Son, content, agreeing!
O love, how strong you are to save,
To put God's Son into his grave,
All people thereby freeing!

Then, when you come before God's throne,
This little lamb shall lead us;
His righteousness shall be our crown,
His innocence precede us.
His grace our dress of royalty;
His all forgiving loyalty
Unites us with our Father,
Where we shall stand at Jesus' side,
His Church, redeemed and glorified,
Where all his faithful gather!

Copyright © 1982 Concordia Publishing House

Ev'ry Year the Christ Child

Ev'ry year the Christ Child
Comes again to earth,
Where his people long for
His redeeming birth;

Coming with his blessing,
Silently, secretly;
Cradled in the softness
Of the heart of me.

All unseen his presence
Walks with me, I know;
Lovingly he leads me
Everywhere I go.

Copyright © Henry L. Lettermann

From Calvary's Cross I Heard Christ Say

From Calvary's cross I heard Christ say:
"Father, forgive these men, for they
In truth know not what they do."
Forgive us too, for often we
In ignorance offend you.

Now to the contrite thief he cries:
"You, truly, will in paradise
Meet me before tomorrow."
Lord, take us soon to heav'n with you,
Who linger in sorrow.

To weeping Mary standing by,
"Behold your son," we hear him cry;
To John, "Behold your mother."
So when we die, let those we leave
In love befriend each other.

The Savior's fourth word was "I thirst!"
O mighty prince of life, your thirst
Yearns for my full salvation.
Your love, your mercy's sacrifice
Compel my adoration.

The fifth, "My God, my God, oh, why
Do you not hear my earnest cry?"
Lord, you were here forsaken
That we may never be so lost;
Let lively faith awaken.

With "It is finished!" you have done,
The course your Father set to run,
The victory achieving.
So let us do your work on earth,
Your promises believing.

At last, as life and suff'rings end:
"O God my Father, I commend
Into your hands my spirit."
Be this, dear Lord, my dying prayer;
O gracious Father, hear it.

Our Lord thus spoke these seven times
When on his cross, for all our crimes,
He died that we not perish.
Let us his last and dying words
In our remembrance cherish.

Copyright © 1982 Concordia Publishing House

Lord Jesus Christ, You Have Prepared

Lord Jesus Christ, you have prepared
This feast for my salvation,
Your very body and your blood;
Thus, at your invitation,
With weary heart, by sin oppressed,
I come to you for needed rest;
I need your peace, your pardon.

Though into heaven you have gone,
Ascending far above me,
Yet here in earthly food I see
How much indeed you love me.
You are not bound to any place;
No contrite heart escapes your grace;
Your love unsought surrounds me.

I eat this bread, I drink this cup,
Your promise firm believing;
In truth your body and your blood
My lips are here receiving.
Your word remains forever true;
All things are possible for you;
Your searching love has found me.
Unaided reason cannot see
What eager faith embraces,
But this consoling supper, Lord,
Each restless doubt displaces.
Your wondrous ways are not confined
Within the limits of my mind;
Your promise wholly triumphs.

I should have died eternally,
But here, repentant kneeling,
Newborn I rise to live the love
Found in your strength, your healing.
Lord, in this sacrament impart
Your joy and courage to my heart;
Dead yet alive I praise you!

Copyright © 1982 Concordia Publishing House

Lord, Open Now My Heart to Hear

Lord, open now my heart to hear,
And through your Word to me draw near;
Preserve that Word in purity
That I your child and heir may be.

Your Word it is that heals my heart,
That makes me whole in ev'ry part;
Your Word of joy within me sings,
True peace and blessedness it brings.

To God the Father, God the Son,
To God the Spirit, Three in One,
Honor and praise forever be
Now and through all eternity!

Copyright © 1982 Concordia Publishing House

Lord, You I Love with All My Heart

Lord, you I love with all my heart;
Oh, let me not from you depart,
With tender mercy cheer me.
Earth has no joy for which I care,
Heaven itself were void and bare
If I can't have you near me.
And should my guilt my heart subdue,
Let nothing shake my trust in you.
You are the portion I desire;
Your sacrifice my soul inspire.
Lord Jesus Christ,
My God and Lord, my God and Lord,
Forsake me not! I trust your Word.

Lord, all I am or have, you gave;
From stubborn ego, Lord you save,
My selfish ways rejecting.
So let me give myself to you,
To all my fellow creatures too,
Your grace, your love reflecting.
Let no false teaching me beguile
Nor Satan's lies my soul defile;
In all my crosses comfort me
That I may bear them patiently.
Lord Jesus Christ,
My God and Lord, my God and Lord,
Let me be yours my soul restored!

Then let at last your angels come,
To Abram's bosom bear me home
That I may die unfearing.
Within my earthen chamber keep
My body safe in peaceful sleep
Until your reappearing.
And then from death awaken me
That my own eyes with joy may see,
O Son of God, your glorious face,
My Savior and my ground of grace!
Lord Jesus Christ,
Oh, hear my prayer; oh, hear my prayer,
Your love surround me ev'rywhere!

Copyright © 1982 Concordia Publishing House

Background Notes

Hymns, Carols and Translations

Abraham's God and Ours
Written: April 1970
Theme: Anniversary
Suggested tune: Original tune by Paul G. Bunjes
Written for the 125th anniversary of St. Lorenz Evangelical Lutheran Church in Frankenmuth, Michigan.

A Carpenter My Father
Written: 1974
Theme: Faith, renewal
Suggested tune: CARPENTER by Melvin W. Block
This text first appeared in the Spring 1975 issue of *Motif*.

America the Blest
Written: 1967
Theme: Patriotism
Written for volume five of the *Concordia Music Education Series* published by Concordia Publishing House in 1967.

An Angel Came to Mary
Written: 1961
Theme: Annunciation
Suggested tune: MAGDALENA
This text first appeared in volume one of the *Concordia Music Education Series* published by Concordia Publishing House in 1961.

And When the Lord Said
Written: 1967
Theme: Christmas
Suggested tune: Original tune by Gerhard C. Becker

As Moses, Lost in Sinai's Wilderness
Written: 1964
Theme: Anniversary
Suggested tune: RIVER FOREST by Richard W. Hillert
This text was written for the centennial of Concordia Teachers College, River Forest, Illinois in 1964.

A Strangely Quiet Bethlehem
Written: 1966
Theme: Christmas
Suggested tune: RADKE by Carl F. Schalk
With original music by Carl Schalk, written for and published in the December 1966 issue of Lutheran Education.

At Evening
Written: 1965
Theme: Evening, protection
Suggested tune: Original tune by Victor Hildner
This text was written for volume two of the *Concordia Music Education Series* published by Concordia Publishing House in 1965.

A White Lily Blows
Written: 1966
Theme: Easter
Suggested tune: Original music written by Richard W. Hillert
With original music by Richard Hillert, written for and published in the April 1966 issue of Lutheran Education.

Best You Sleep Now, Little Jesus
Written: 1972
Theme: Christmas

Suggested tune: LULLABY by Carl Schalk
This carol was written for "Celebrate the Joy of His Birth," a supplement to Motif, December 1972.

Birthday Greeting
Written: 1961
Theme: Birthday celebration
Suggested tune: Original tune by A. H. Kahlenberg
This text was written for volume one of the *Concordia Music Education Series* published by Concordia Publishing House in 1961.

Caught in the Storm of Earth's Uncertain Life
Written: 1972
Theme: Restoration
Suggested tune: ES WOLLE GOTT UNS GENAEDIG SEIN
This text was written for the Spring 1972 issue of *Motif.*

Chickadee
Written: 1967
Theme: Children
This text was written for volume six of the *Concordia Music Education Series* published by Concordia Publishing House in 1967.

Christ Our King
Written: 1962
Theme: Christmas
Suggested tune: Original tune by Richard W. Hillert
Written for the Spring 1962 issue of *Motif.*

Continually Triumphant Seraphim
Written: 1962
Theme: Praise and adoration
Suggested tune: TRIUMPHANT SERAPHIM by Richard W. Hillert
With music by Richard Hillert, selected for the National Convention of the Lutheran Church—Missouri Synod, Cleveland, Ohio, 1962.

Dear Father, Lord of All
Written: Date unknown
Theme: Anniversary, consecration
Suggested tune: DARWALL'S 148th
Written for the 25th anniversary of Holy Cross Lutheran Church, Dallas Texas.

I Am Jesus' Letter
Written: 1961
Theme: Missions, children's evangelism
Suggested tune: Original tune by Victor Hildner
This text was written for volume one of the *Concordia Music Education Series* published by Concordia Publishing House in 1961.

Injun Summer
Written: 1967
Theme: Children
Written for volume five of the *Concordia Music Education Series* published by Concordia Publishing House in 1967.

In Little Bethlehem
Written: 1984
Theme: Christmas
Suggested Tune: Original tune by Richard W. Hillert
Written for and published by Lutheran Education, November-December 1984.

In the Morning
Written: 1967
Theme: Children
Written for volume five of the *Concordia Music Education Series* published by Concordia Publishing House in 1967.

In the Winter
Written: 1967
Theme: Children
Written for volume five of the *Concordia Music Education Series* published by Concordia Publishing House in 1967.

I Wonder, I Wonder
Written: 1966
Theme: Creation, new life
Suggested tune: ITALIAN FOLK SONG
Written for volume four of the *Concordia Music Education Series* published by Concordia Publishing House in 1966.

Lead Us, Lord
Written: 1976
Theme: A hymn for the United States Bicentennial
Suggested tune: Original tune by Richard W. Hillert
Written for and published by *Lutheran Education*, January-February 1976.

Like Sea and Air and Sky
Written: 1983
Theme: Christian education
Suggested tune: Original tune written by Werner P. Grams

Lord, Bless the Manger-Child
Written: 1974
Theme: Christmas
Suggested tune: Original tune by Ralph C. Schultz
With original music by Ralph Schultz, published in 1976 in "Bless the Manger Child" published by Concordia Publishing House.

Lord God, Reform Our Hearts
Written: 1967
Theme: Reformation
Suggested tune: Original tune by Carl F. Schalk
With original music by Carl Schalk, written for and published in the October 1967 issue of *Lutheran Education* to commemorate the 450th anniversary of the Lutheran Reformation in 1967.

Lord Jesus Christ, the Children's Friend
Written: 1980
Theme: Christian elementary education
Suggested tune: TALLIS' CANON
Written as a hymn on Christian education for the publication of *Lutheran Worship* (1982).

Morning Round
Written: 1967
Theme: Children
Written for volume five of the *Concordia Music Education Series* published by Concordia Publishing House in 1967.

Mount Rushmore USA
Written: 1967
Theme: Children
Written for volume five of the *Concordia Music Education Series* published by Concordia Publishing House in 1967.

Northwest Passage
Written: 1967
Theme: Children
Written for volume five of the *Concordia Music Education Series* published by Concordia Publishing House in 1967.

Not with the Strength
Written: 1967
Theme: Anniversary
Suggested tune: Original tune by Paul G. Bunjes
Written for the 125th anniversary of Trinity Lutheran Church in Saint Joseph, Michigan.

Old Man Mississippi
Written: 1967
Theme: Children
Written for volume five of the *Concordia Music Education Series* published by Concordia Publishing House in 1967.

On Christmas Morning Children Sing
Written: 1983
Theme: Christmas
Suggested tune: AARON MICHAEL by Carl F. Schalk
With music by Carl Schalk, written for and published in the December 1983 issue of *Lutheran Education*.

On Galilee's High Mountain
Written: ca. 1980
Theme: Missions
Suggested tune: MISSIONARY HYMN by Lowell Mason
Written at the request of the Hymn Texts and Music Committee of the LCMS Commission on Worship for inclusion in *Lutheran Worship* (1982).

Our Father, Who from Heaven Above
Written: ca. 1980
Theme: Prayer
Suggested tune: VATER UNSER by Martin Luther
Fred Precht wrote the following in *Lutheran Worship: Hymnal Companion*, "The nine-stanza length of Martin Luther's metrical paraphrase of the Lord's Prayer (LW 431) prompted the Commission on Worship to include in *Lutheran Worship* (1982) this three-stanza version of Henry Lettermann. In examining it and noting its laudable qualities one cannot but agree with the old saying, "*In der Beschrankung zeigt sich der Meister*" ("In exercising restraint, one shows himself/herself to be a master").

Our Savior Kindly Calls
Written: 1961
Theme: Trust, forgiveness
Suggested tune: FRANCONIA
Written for and published in volume one of the *Concordia Music Education Series* published by Concordia Publishing House in 1961.

Prayer
Written: 1967
Theme: Children
Written for volume five of the *Concordia Music Education Series* published by Concordia Publishing House in 1967.

St. Luke: The Gentile Stranger
Written: 1968
Theme: Witness, rededication
Suggested tune: "MUEHLHAUSEN MELODIENBUCH"
Written for and published in volume five of the *Concordia Music Education Series* published by Concordia Publishing House in 1968.

Softly, Softly, Sleep Jesus
Written: Date unknown
Theme: Christmas
Suggested tune: Original tune by Ralph C. Schultz

Song of the Liberty Bell
Written: 1967
Theme: Children
Written for volume five of the *Concordia Music Education Series* published by Concordia Publishing House in 1967.

So Shall Our Song of Praise
Written: 1960
Theme: Praise
Suggested tune: DOXOLOGY by Richard W. Hillert
Used as DOXOLOGY in "Cantata No. 2" (work in progress, 1960)
Music by Richard Hillert.

Spring Is Springing
Written: 1967
Theme: Creation
Suggested tune: Original tune by Leslie Zeddies
Written for volume five of the *Concordia Music Education Series* published by Concordia Publishing House in 1967.

Still Are the Hills
Written: 1972
Theme: Christmas
Suggested tune: SLANE
Published in 1973 by Concordia Publishing House as an anthem for mixed voices by Paul Bouman.

Still, Still, Wind and Will
Written: ca.1951
Theme: Christmas
Suggested tune: No extant tune

That We Might Believe
Written: 1960
Theme: A text for a cantata
Suggested tune: No extant tune
First published in the Fall 1960 issue of *Motif*.

The Black of Night in Bethlehem
Written: 1964
Theme: Christmas
Suggested tune: Original tune by Richard W. Hillert
This carol was written for the November 1964 issue of *Lutheran Education*.

The Children of the Faith
Written: 1967
Theme: Faith
Suggested tune: CHILDREN OF FAITH by Richard W. Hillert
With music composed by Richard Hillert, commissioned for the dedication of the new catechism at the National Convention of the Lutheran Church—Missouri Synod, New York City, 1967.

The Christ-Child King
Written: 1986
Theme: Christmas
Suggested Tune: Original tune by Richard W. Hillert

Written for and published by *CHRISTMAS, The Annual of Christmas Literature and Art*, volume 57, Augsburg Publishing House, 1986.

The Great Puddles
Written: 1967
Theme: Children
Written for volume five of the *Concordia Music Education Series* published by Concordia Publishing House in 1967.

The Judas Tree
Written: 1962
Theme: Renewal
Suggested tune: No extant tune
Written for the Winter 1962 issue of *Motif*.

The Lord Be Your Shepherd
Written: 1966
Theme: Trust
Suggested tune: SCANDINAVIAN FOLK SONG
Written for volume four of the *Concordia Music Education Series* published by Concordia Publishing House in 1966.

The Lord Is My Light
Written: 1971
Theme: Psalm 27
Suggested tune: Original tune by Heinz Werner Zimmermann
Dr. Lettermann provided alternate texts for stanzas 2-4 in this setting by Heinz Werner Zimmermann. The subsequent setting was published in "Five Hymns" by Heinz Werner Zimmermann published by Concordia Publishing House in 1971.

The Lord's My Shepherd, Leading Me
Written: ca.1980
Theme: Psalm 23
Suggested tune: BROTHER JAMES' AIR
Written at the request of the LCMS Commission on Worship for inclusion in *Lutheran Worship* (1982).

The Name of Jesus Sweetly Sounds
Written: 1977
Theme: The Presentation of Our Lord
Suggested tune: SIMEON by Carl F. Schalk
With music by Carl Schalk, this text was written for and published by *Lutheran Education* in December 1977.

The Precious Gift
Written: 1962
Theme: Christmas
Suggested tune: Original tune by Ralph C. Schultz
With original music by Ralph Schultz, written for and published in the November 1962 issue of *Lutheran Education*.

The Wind of the Sea
Written: 1967
Theme: Children
Written for volume five of the *Concordia Music Education Series* published by Concordia Publishing House in 1967.

This Is the Cross of Christ
Written: 1977
Theme: Lent
Suggested tune: Original tune by Richard W. Hillert
With music by Richard Hillert, written for and published in the March-April 1977 issue of *Lutheran Education*.

Watchman on the Wall of Zion
Written: 1982
Theme: Advent
Suggested tune: SANDRA by Werner P. Grams
With music by Werner Grams, written for the November-December 1982 issue of *Lutheran Education*.

What News This Bitter Night
Written: 1962
Theme: Christmas

Suggested tune: Original tune by Richard W. Hillert
With original music by Richard Hillert, written for and published in the November 1962 issue of *Lutheran Education.*

When Time Is Full, the Stars Ignite
Written: 1976
Theme: Advent
Suggested tune: Original tune by Carl F. Schalk
With original music by Carl Schalk, written for and published in the November-December 1976 issue of *Lutheran Education.*

Who Are These That Earnest Knock
Written: 1957
Theme: Christmas
Suggested tune: DIES EST LAETITIAE
Written in 1957 for a chapel service at Concordia Teachers College, River Forest, Illinois.

Who Found America
Written: 1967
Theme: Children
Written for volume five of the *Concordia Music Education Series* published by Concordia Publishing House in 1967.

With Flame of Might
Written: 1966
Theme: Saint Michael and All Angels
Suggested tune: FLAME OF MIGHT by Carl F. Schalk
This carol for St. Michael and All Angels was written for *Spirit* magazine and first appeared in the September 1966 issue of that publication.

Translations of German Hymns

A Lamb Alone Bears Willingly
Written: ca.1980
Theme: Passion Week
Translation of: "*Ein Lammlein geht und tragt die Schuld*" by Paul Gerhardt ca. 1648
Suggested tune: AN WASSERFLÜSSEN BABYLON
This translation was prepared at the request of the Hymn Text and Music Committee of the LCMS Commission on Worship for *Lutheran Worship* (1982).

Ev'ry Year the Christ Child
Written: 1981
Theme: Christmas
Translation from: "*Alle Jahre Wieder*" by Johann Wilhelm Hey, 1789-1854.
Suggested tune: ALLE JAHRE WIEDER by Friedrich Silcher, 1789-1860
This text appeared in a setting by Carl Halter in the November-December 1981 issue of *Lutheran Education*.

From Calvary's Cross I Heard Christ Say
Written: ca.1980
Theme: Passion Week
Translation of: "*Da Jesus an dem Kreuze stund*" by Johann Boschenstain ca. 1515
Suggested tune: DA JESUS AN DES KREUZES
This translation was prepared at the request of the Hymn Text and Music Committee of the LCMS Commission on Worship for *Lutheran Worship* (1982).

Lord Jesus Christ, You Have Prepared
Written: ca. 1977
Theme: The Lord's Supper
Translation of: "*Herr Jesu Christ, du hast bereit't*" by Samuel Kinner ca. 1638

Suggested tune: DU LEBENSBROT, HERR JESU CHRIST by Peter Sohren ca. 1668

Lord, Open Now My Heart to Hear
Written: ca. 1980
Theme: Beginning of service
Translation of: "*Herr, offne mir die Herzenstur*" by Johannes Olearius ca. 1671
Suggested tune: ERHALT UNS, HERR
This translation was also prepared at the request of the Hymn Text and Music Committee of the LCMS Commission on Worship for *Lutheran Worship* (1982).

Lord, You I Love with All My Heart
Written: ca.1980
Theme: Trust
Translation of: "*Herzlich lieb hab' ich dich, o Herr*" by Martin Schalling in 1571
Suggested tune: HERZLICH LIEB
This translation was prepared at the request of the Hymn Text and Music Committee of the LCMS Commission on Worship for *Lutheran Worship* (1982).

Index of Titles and First Lines

Original Hymns, Carols, Sacred Texts, and Secular Poems

Abraham's God and Ours............29
A Carpenter My Father 30
America the Blest 32
An Angel Came to Mary..............33
And When the Lord Said 34
As Moses, Lost in
 Sinai's Wilderness....................35
A Strangely Quiet Bethlehem 36
At Evening 37
A White Lily Blows 38
Best You Sleep Now,
 Little Jesus...............................39
Birthday Greeting........................40
Caught in the Storm of Earth's
 Uncertain Life 41
Chickadee 43
Christ Our King 44
Continually Triumphant
 Seraphim..................................45
Dear Father, Lord of All..............46
I Am Jesus' Letter........................47
Injun Summer 48
In Little Bethlehem 49
In the Morning............................50
In the Winter...............................51
I Wonder, I Wonder....................52
Lead Us, Lord 53
Like Sea and Air and Sky 54
Lord, Bless the Manger-Child.....55
Lord God, Reform Our Hearts...56
Lord Jesus Christ, the
 Children's Friend.....................57
Morning Round..........................58
Mount Rushmore, USA...............59
Northwest Passage 60
Not with the Strength.................61
Old Man Mississippi 62
On Christmas Morning
 Children Sing 63
On Galilee's High Mountain.......64
Our Father, Who from
 Heaven Above 66
Our Savior Kindly Calls 67
Prayer..68
St. Luke: The Gentile Stranger...69
Softly, Softly, Sleep Jesus 70
Song of the Liberty Bell...............71
So Shall Our Song of Praise 72
Spring Is Springing 73
Still Are the Hills 74

Still, Still, Wind and Will 75
That We Might Believer 76
The Black of Night
  in Bethlehem 79
The Children of the Faith 80
The Christ-Child King 81
The Great Puddles 82
The Judas Tree 83
The Lord Be Your Shepherd 86
The Lord Is My Light 87
The Lord's My Shepherd,
  Leading Me 88
The Name of Jesus
  Sweetly Sounds 89
The Precious Gift 90
The Wind of the Sea 91
This Is the Cross of Christ 92
Watchmen on the Wall of Zion .. 93
What News This Bitter Night 94
When Time Is Full,
  the Stars Ignite 95
Who Are These That
  Earnest Knock 96
Who Found America 97
With Flame of Might 98

Translations of German Hymns

A Lamb Alone Bears
  Willingly 101
Ev'ry Year the Christ Child 103
From Calvary's Cross I
  Heard Christ Say 104
Lord Jesus Christ, You
  Have Prepared 106
Lord, Open Now My Heart
  to Hear 108
Lord, You I Love with
  All My Heart 109